Worship Feast

20 Complete Services in the Spirit of Taizé

Contents

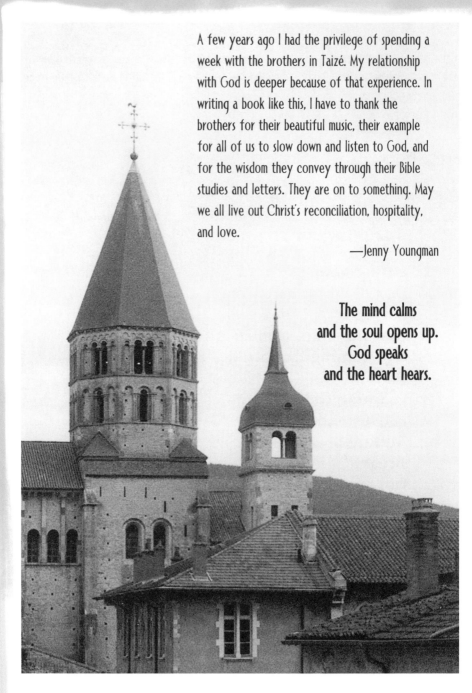

A few years ago I had the privilege of spending a week with the brothers in Taizé. My relationship with God is deeper because of that experience. In writing a book like this, I have to thank the brothers for their beautiful music, their example for all of us to slow down and listen to God, and for the wisdom they convey through their Bible studies and letters. They are on to something. May we all live out Christ's reconciliation, hospitality, and love.

—Jenny Youngman

**The mind calms
and the soul opens up.
God speaks
and the heart hears.**

The Spirit of Taizé

On a hill in southern France, you'll find a community of brothers that has opened its door to the world as an act of hospitality. Young people from around the world flock to Taizé to be near the brothers, to pray, to be silent, to be simple, to be faithful. But what is it about this place that draws the youth of the world? Surely there are plenty of other more interesting vacation spots.

Youth come seeking the space—external and internal—in which to meet God. Their lives (and ours) are so wrapped up in to-do lists (on which one would find items such as church, youth group, Bible study, and so on) that we seldom find the space or the clarity to simply listen to the voice of God speaking deep into our hearts. That's what goes on at Taizé—the freedom and space to hear God's voice.

Time in Taizé is more like a melodic, holy rhythm than the frenzied pace of everyday life. Three times a day visitors are called to prayer by the chiming of bells. The prayers are not like ordinary prayer meetings or worship services. Instead of coming together to talk *to* God, the community gathers to *listen*. Instead of talking about the Scripture, the Scripture is read and left to speak for itself in the silence. By singing simple songs of prayer over and over again, the mind calms and the soul opens up; God speaks and the heart hears.

So how does that sense of holy ground that has drawn thousands of youth from all over the world translate into our youth rooms, prayer chapels, and ministry settings? What can we do to emulate the spirit that is so evident in Taizé? We can start by creating sacred spaces in our programs to listen to God. Instead of blaring music 24/7, we can light some candles and pray together in song. Instead of working up a great talk, we can read Scripture and sit together in silent prayer.

Of course, that is not to say that this style of worship is the only way. I love exciting praise music, and youth sermons are must-haves for youth groups and always will be. However, I hope you will accept the challenge of creating quiet space in your youth programs for youth to learn the art of hearing God. It takes time and patience, but God longs to speak to us—if we can stop talking long enough to listen. Give your young people the blessing of silence, and encourage them to not be afraid of it but to embrace it as time to hear God's voice.

Peace be with you.

How to Use the Services

The services in this book are for you to experience the style and spirit of Taizé.
Let the Spirit guide you as you pray together. Use the printed service as a basic guideline. If you want to rearrange things or use different songs, feel free. You'll want to create an authentic worship experience for your community. Permission is granted for you to photocopy the services, so if you want to use them "as is," just print and hand them out.

The Space

Create a different space from your usual setting. Light candles, burn incense, sit on the floor, or kneel around an altar with a cross or other artwork displayed. Involve the youth in creating the altar. If you have some youth who are artists, ask them to paint depictions of various biblical scenes and characters and use them as altar stations. Make the space smell, feel, and look different from usual.

The Songs

All of the songs come from the Taizé community. However, it is perfectly appropriate to incorporate other songs familiar to the youth, or even songs they have written. Avoid "up-front" leadership by having the song leader and musicians sit behind or among the group. The songs should be sung over and over, at least four to eight times each, so that they become deeply felt prayers. Allow the song leader and accompanist to decide when to move on to the next song.

The Worship Feast Taizé Songbook

Each song used in the services is listed by its corresponding number in the *Worship Feast Taizé Songbook*. You'll want to have a Songbook for each participant. Each song includes a melody line and simple guitar chords. Make sure your musicians practice the songs ahead of time for smooth transitions.

Because the Taizé community is a place of reconciliation and true community, most songs are translated into various languages. English, French, Spanish, and Latin translations are printed in the Songbook. Encourage your group to sing in whatever language they feel comfortable. Multiple languages may be sung at the same time—the same way it happens in Taizé.

The Worship Feast Taizé CD

In the back of this book, you'll find a split-track CD that includes all of the songs used in the Services and the Songbook. Use the CD to learn the songs with the voices, and then use instrumental versions as accompaniment to your services. You'll probably find that you will just want to listen to the CD in your office or car. Each song is sung through five times. The recordings are simple versions of the songs. The last two tracks provide samples of what might be done if you allow your group to add its own twist, making the songs their own.

The Scriptures

Have volunteers read the Scriptures from their seats without drawing attention to themselves. Encourage readers to practice. In the spirit of Taizé, invite individuals to read aloud in other languages, including sign language.

Something to Think About in the Silence

Each service has a short meditation that you may or may not want to use in your prayer service. If your youth have a hard time settling down for the silence, use the meditation as something they can think about or let God talk to them about. These can be read aloud or silently.

Another option is to set up creative stations to help the youth focus in the silence. Provide some art supplies and writing materials around the room. Make sure each participant has enough space to work without distracting others.

The Silence

You may not be able to have a period of ten to fifteen minutes of silence, but even a few minutes are valuable. If your youth aren't used to extended quiet times, start small and work your way up to ten minutes or so. When you're ready, try for up to fifteen minutes.

The Prayers

Use the written prayers to conclude the silence or close your service. If you have a set time for the service to begin and end, a prayer gives a sense of closure. However, if you have the freedom, let the youth leave as they feel led during the last song.

Loving With Your Life

Opening Songs

"Bless the Lord," No. 1
"In God Alone" (Mon âme se repose), No. 5
"O Lord, Hear My Prayer," No. 11

Scripture Reading   1 Corinthians 13:1-8a

"If I speak in the tongues of mortals and of angels, but do not have love, I am a noisy gong or a clanging cymbal. And if I have prophetic powers, and understand all mysteries and all knowledge, and if I have all faith, so as to remove mountains, but do not have love, I am nothing. If I give away all my possessions, and if I hand over my body so that I may boast, but do not have love, I gain nothing. Love is patient; love is kind; love is not envious or boastful or arrogant or rude. It does not insist on its own way; it is not irritable or resentful; it does not rejoice in wrongdoing, but rejoices in the truth. It bears all things, believes all things, hopes all things, endures all things. Love never ends."

Something to Think About in the Silence

When was the last time you really loved someone? I don't mean when was the last time you were in love, but when have you really and truly shown love to another person? What does your life tell others about God's love?

What we learn from Paul in 1 Corinthians is that love is not cheap or easy and that there is no substitute for God's love on earth. We can have every worldly indulgence, or the most beautiful poetic tongue, or a sense of prophecy, but when these things are void of God, they are nothing. Even our bodies are nothing if they are not temples for God.

For some of us, the reason we don't let our lives tell others about God's love is that we haven't truly experienced God's love deep in our hearts. Sure, we know all the verses about love, and we know that "God so loved the world . . . ." But we don't really know what that love means for our lives. Think about it: When was the last time that you really knew—deep in your heart—that you are loved by God?

The answer to this question may not be easy, but it directly affects our showing love to others. If our lives say that we are completely caught up in God's love, then we will stand up for what is right and be a voice for those who cannot speak. If our lives say that we know God's love, then we will be compassionate and merciful. These are the ways that we show love to others—by being patient, kind, humble, respectful, selfless, and honest. If we do not live God's love, then we are nothing but noise in the world—like static on the TV. This Scripture passage isn't just for weddings and married people. All of us are called to love one another in this way—married or not.

Read the Scripture passage again. In the silence, let God tell you that God loves you. Experience that love. Listen for the ways in which God is telling you to love others.

Prayer: "God whose love never ends, envelope us in your love. Let it so fill us that we then live out a love that is patient and kind and forever. Thank you for loving us. We want to learn to love you more. Amen."

Closing Songs

"Lord Jesus Christ" (Jésus le Christ), No. 9
"In the Lord" (El Senyor), No. 6

2 Losing Your Life

Opening Songs

"Sing Praises" (Laudate omnes gentes), No. 13
"Come and Fill" (Confitemini Domino), No. 3
"Wait for the Lord," No. 15

Scripture Reading   Mark 8:34-38

"He called the crowd with his disciples, and said to them, 'If any want to become my followers, let them deny themselves and take up their cross and follow me. For those who want to save their life will lose it, and those who lose their life for my sake, and for the sake of the gospel, will save it. For what will it profit them to gain the whole world and forfeit their life? Indeed, what can they give in return for their life? Those who are ashamed of me and of my words in this adulterous and sinful generation, of them the Son of Man will also be ashamed when he comes in the glory of his Father with the holy angels.'"

Something to Think About in the Silence

What does it mean to gain the whole world only to lose your soul? Think about that for a minute.

Jesus desires a close relationship with each of us. So close in fact that we would be willing to give up our possessions—even our lives—to follow him. In the few verses prior to this particular Scripture passage, Jesus asks Peter who others say he is. Then Jesus asks Peter, "Who do *you* say that I am?" Jesus uses this question as the basis for what it means to follow him. If we say that Jesus is the Messiah, then we have no choice but to follow him. If we choose to follow Jesus the Messiah, then we are required to give up our lives for his sake.

Who do you say that Jesus is? Is he your Savior? your friend? your Messiah? Surely he is all of these and more. And because of that, we are called to lay down our lives to gain his. When you think about it, we pay a lot of attention to a million different things throughout our lives. How much attention do you pay to your soul? In other words, how is it with your soul? Have you laid down your life to follow Christ?

Following Jesus is the one thing that really matters in this world. If you were to make a list describing your day-to-day activities, most of it would add up to nothing without Christ. What do you need to "lay down" in your life to truly follow Christ? Your love of money? Your time? Your ego?

In the remaining silence, examine what may be crowding Christ out of your life. Clear out the things that are keeping you from fully surrendering to his call. Jesus requires no less than to be the Lord of your life. Will you follow him?

Prayer: "Giver of all good things, help us to lay down our lives and follow your Son Jesus Christ. Teach us that without you we have nothing. You alone are worthy of our very lives, and we offer them to you in the name of Christ our Lord. Amen."

Closing Songs

"Nothing Can Trouble" (Nada te turbe), No. 10
"Let Your Servant Now Go in Peace" (Nunc Dimittis), No. 8

3 Don't Worry; Have Peace

Opening Songs

"In God Alone" (Mon âme se repose), No. 5
"Our Darkness" (La ténèbre), No. 12
"Come and Fill" (Confitemini Domino), No. 3

Scripture Reading   Philippians 4:4-7

"Rejoice in the Lord always; again I will say, Rejoice. Let your gentleness be known to everyone. The Lord is near. Do not worry about anything, but in everything by prayer and supplication with thanksgiving let your requests be made known to God. And the peace of God, which surpasses all understanding, will guard your hearts and your minds in Christ Jesus."

Something to Think About in the Silence

I don't know about you, but I cannot imagine what it would be like to not worry about anything. It seems like an impossible feat, and yet that is the instruction from Philippians. Think back to Jesus teaching us about worry in the Book of Matthew. He tells us that God cares for the lilies of the field and the littlest sparrow. How much more does God care for each one of us? Take a minute right now to think about that one truth. God cares for the tiniest sparrow—how much more must God care for you!

What do you worry about? School? Work? Money? Family issues? Relationships? Our minds and hearts are inclined to worry about things that don't matter in the long run. What a wonderful promise we have in this Bible passage. When our worries are submitted to the compassionate and loving hands of God, we experience the peace of God in our hearts and minds. Our hearts are guarded and protected by God's peace, and our worrying will be no more. Take a few minutes to think about what it means to have a peace that guards the heart and the mind.

Think about how often we say to one another: "Oh, don't worry about it. You'll be fine." Do we just respond: "OK. You're right. I won't worry about it"? Of course not. We say "OK." But then we continue worrying. This Scripture says "Don't worry" in an authoritative way. This is God saying to us: "Don't worry about it. You'll be fine. I'm here."

Listen to your heart now and hear God whispering this Scripture passage in your heart. "Rejoice my beloved child. Relax. I am right here with you. Don't worry. Just tell me what you need. Rely on me; I will not fail you. I will protect you and fill you with my peace."

Sung Response

"In the Lord" (El Senyor), No. 6

Prayer: "God of peace and love, take away our worries. You promise to guard our hearts and minds in Christ Jesus, so we open ourselves to your protection. Help us come to know you in such a way that we willingly surrender our worries to your loving hands. May the peace that surpasses all understanding live in our hearts and minds. Amen."

Closing Songs

"Sing Praises" (Laudate omnes gentes), No. 13
"Let Your Servant Now Go in Peace" (Nunc Dimittis), No. 8

Loving the Least

Opening Songs

"In God Alone" (Mon âme se repose), No. 5
"Our Darkness" (La ténèbre), No. 12
"By Night" (De noche iremos), No. 2

Scripture Reading   Matthew 25:34-37

"Then the king will say to those at his right hand, 'Come, you that are blessed by my Father, inherit the kingdom prepared for you from the foundation of the world; for I was hungry and you gave me food, I was thirsty and you gave me something to drink, I was a stranger and you welcomed me, I was naked and you gave me clothing, I was sick and you took care of me, I was in prison and you visited me.'"

Something to Think About in the Silence

God's love knows no limits. Christian love sees no boundaries or divisions and is not discriminating. In the kingdom of God, love is free. People are never too busy or uncomfortable to love another.

When you imagine someone who is hungry, thirsty, a stranger, naked, sick, or in prison, whom do you see? Put a face with each of those images and reflect on that for a minute. Probably we all can think of times when someone has needed us—our time, our money, our excess, our friendship—yet we just went on our way and paid no attention. Or worse still, we paid attention but chose not to help.

The kingdom of God does not allow a kind of love that picks and chooses or a love that does not give to or make time for those in need. Christ teaches us that what we feel towards and how we treat even the least among us in today's world is equal to our love for him. If we do not show kindness and compassion to every individual with whom we come in contact, we are not bearing the face of Christ in the world. Think about these questions as you sit in the silence:

When have you seen Christ hungry and in need of some food?

When have you seen Christ thirsty and in need of a drink?

When have you seen Christ in the face of a stranger?

When have you seen Christ in need of clothes?

When have you seen Christ in prison or sick and in need of companionship?

Let the love of Christ so fill your heart today that it will spill out into the world. So many people need the giving love of Christ. How will you share it?

Prayer: "In Christ our every need is met. Christ provides. We offer ourselves for the sake of meeting the needs of all God's children on earth so that one day we might live in a world where no one goes hungry or thirsty, or feels estranged, or lives alone. Come with your love, Lord Jesus. Come. Amen."

Closing Songs

"Nothing Can Trouble" (Nada te turbe), No. 10
"Jesus, Remember Me," No. 7

5 Fearfully and Wonderfully Made

Opening Songs

"Lord Jesus Christ" (Jésus le Christ), No. 9
"Bless the Lord," No. 1
"O Lord, Hear My Prayer," No. 11

Scripture Reading   Psalm 139:1-6, 13-14, 23-24

"O Lord, you have searched me and known me. You know when I sit down and when I rise up; you discern my thoughts from far away. You search out my path and my lying down, and are acquainted with all my ways. Even before a word is on my tongue, O Lord, you know it completely. You hem me in, behind and before, and lay your hand upon me. Such knowledge is too wonderful for me; it is so high that I cannot attain it. . . . For it was you who formed my inward parts; you knit me together in my mother's womb. I praise you, for I am fearfully and wonderfully made. Wonderful are your works; that I know very well. . . . Search me, O God, and know my heart; test me and know my thoughts. See if there is any wicked way in me, and lead me in the way everlasting."

Something to Think About in the Silence

God knows each of us personally and is familiar with all our ways. God knows us so intimately that our thoughts cannot be hidden. Imagine being "hemmed in behind and before" and "knitted together" like a grandmother sewing a special blanket for a precious grandchild. What a beautiful image of our loving God, crafting and creating each of us as beloved children.

Do you have days when you feel less than God's beloved child? God hears your cries. Do you ever feel alone—like no one in the world understands you? God knows you better than you know yourself.

This God is not one who will use knowledge against you.

Have you ever felt like every way you turn is the wrong way? God is there to guide you.

This loving God longs for a relationship with us. Our Creator wants to satisfy our longings, hold us close, and be there for us right when we call.

The psalmist praises God for this unattainable knowledge. God's works are indeed so wonderful. Imagine what it means to be fearfully and wonderfully made. With wonder and reverence, each of us was handcrafted.

In the remaining silence, choose one of the phrases in the Scripture and repeat it—over and over again—until your heart fully believes it. Listen closely as God whispers to you how wonderfully unique and special you are. You are fearfully and wonderfully made.

Prayer: "Loving and creating Lord, search us now. Know our every thought. Remove the voices that tell us we are not special enough, worthy enough, beautiful enough. For you created us to be awesome, wonderful, perfectly unique creations. Remind us that you designed us to be just who we are and not who the world would have us to be. Continue to create in and through us. Your works are wonderful. Amen."

Closing Songs

"In the Lord" (El Senyor), No. 6
"In God Alone" (Mon âme se repose), No. 5

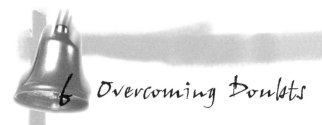

Overcoming Doubts

Opening Songs

"Sing Praises" (Laudate omnes gentes), No. 13
"In God Alone" (Mon âme se repose), No. 5
"Come and Fill" (Confitemini Domino), No. 3

Scripture Reading   John 20:24-29

"But Thomas (who was called the Twin), one of the twelve, was not with them when Jesus came. So the other disciples told him, 'We have seen the Lord.' But he said to them, 'Unless I see the mark of the nails in his hands, and put my finger in the mark of the nails and my hand in his side, I will not believe.' A week later his disciples were again in the house, and Thomas was with them. Although the doors were shut, Jesus came and stood among them and said, 'Peace be with you.' Then he said to Thomas, 'Put your finger here and see my hands. Reach out your hand and put it in my side. Do not doubt but believe.' Thomas answered, 'My Lord and my God!' Jesus said to him, 'Have you believed because you have seen me? Blessed are those who have not seen and yet have come to believe.'

Something to Think About in the Silence

Sometimes Thomas is called "Doubting Thomas," but I think he got a bad wrap. I honestly think I would have reacted exactly as he did if my friends had come to tell me that my leader had come back from the dead—with the scars to prove it. Surely the other disciples did not believe fully right away, but Thomas comes to be known as "Doubting Thomas" because of his disbelief. How do you think you would have reacted to that news?

But Jesus, in his compassionate way, helped Thomas with his doubt and led him to belief. He told Thomas to touch and feel that it was truly him. I wonder if Thomas actually did believe, but to him, somehow the news was just too good to be true. Have you ever wanted to believe something with your whole heart but worried that it was too good to be true? Put yourself in Thomas' place. Hear Jesus say to you: "Put your fingers here and see my hands. Put your hand in my side. It is me."

Jesus says that those who believe without seeing are blessed. Do you believe without seeing? Or are you one who needs to see and touch the wounds? Jesus didn't love Thomas any less because he needed proof. Jesus doesn't love us any less when we need extra assurance of his presence with us. Surely it is better to ask and receive than to live permanently in doubt and unbelief.

In the remaining silence, reflect on the strength of your belief. Examine your heart and submit to God what it is that keeps you from one-hundred-percent belief.

Prayer

One: Hear our prayer, O Lord.
All: Lord Jesus Christ, let not our doubts speak to us.
One: Help our unbelief and cause us to have the faith that believes without seeing.
All: Lord Jesus Christ, let not our doubts speak to us.
One: When we doubt, take our hands and place them on your wounds.
All: Lord Jesus Christ, let not our doubts speak to us.
One: Show yourself to us again and again, not because we don't believe, but because sometimes our humanness tells us that you are too good to be true.
All: Lord Jesus Christ, let not our doubts speak to us. My Lord and My God! Amen.

Closing Song

"Lord Jesus Christ" (Jésus le Christ), No. 9

Thirsting for God

Opening Songs

"Sing Praises" (Laudate omnes gentes), No. 13
"Glory to God" (Gloria), No. 4
"Bless the Lord," No. 1

Scripture Reading   Psalm 63:1-4, 8

"O God, you are my God, I seek you, my soul thirsts for you; my flesh faints for you, as in a dry and weary land where there is no water. So I have looked upon you in the sanctuary, beholding your power and glory. Because your steadfast love is better than life, my lips will praise you. So I will bless you as long as I live; I will lift up my hands and call on your name. . . . My soul clings to you; your right hand upholds me."

Something to Think About in the Silence

God's love is so amazing. Have you ever been so caught up in God's love that all you knew to do was cry out in praise? The psalmist makes the comparison of needing God so badly with being stranded in a desert with no water. He knows of God's goodness, so he vows to praise, bless, and cling to God as God holds him up. This is a person who fully believes that God will provide for every need, and because of that, God is worthy of praise.

Imagine your soul thirsting for God. Look at the image on the next page and meditate on God filling your thirsty soul with living water.

Prayer: "O God, you are our God. Your love continually amazes us. Be honored by our praises and the way we live our lives. Fill our thirsty souls with your living water. Amen."

Closing Songs

"By Night" (De noche iremos), No. 2
"In the Lord" (El Senyor), No. 6

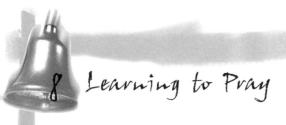

Learning to Pray

Opening Songs

"Bless the Lord," No. 1
"Wait for the Lord," No. 15
"O Lord, Hear My Prayer," No. 11

Scripture Reading   Luke 11:1-4, 9-10, 13

"He was praying in a certain place, and after he had finished, one of his disciples said to him,
'Lord, teach us to pray, as John taught his disciples.' He said to them, 'When you pray, say:
Father, hallowed be your name. Your kingdom come. Give us each day our daily bread. And
forgive us our sins, for we ourselves forgive everyone indebted to us. And do not bring us to
the time of trial. . . . So I say to you, Ask, and it will be given you; search, and you will find;
knock, and the door will be opened for you. For everyone who asks receives, and everyone
who searches finds, and for everyone who knocks, the door will be opened. . . .
If you . . . know how to give good gifts to your children, how much more will the heavenly
Father give the Holy Spirit to those who ask him!'"

Something to Think About in the Silence

Prayer is a such an important part of our faith, and yet it is one of the most difficult
disciplines to practice. In this passage, we see that even the disciples were unsure of exactly
how to pray. Sometimes we are afraid of seeming selfish by asking for too much. Other times
we worry that we're not praying enough.

Sometimes we're afraid to pray aloud in front of others, but when we pray alone, we end up
falling asleep or realize our mind is wandering.

Why is prayer so difficult when Jesus gave us the exact words to say? He says that everyone who asks receives. God wants to shower us with blessings and answers to our prayers, but still we don't commit ourselves to the practice of prayer.

What is your prayer life like? Are you satisfied with the time you spend in prayer, or do you desire a deeper prayer life? What is standing in the way of that deeper sense of prayer? Jesus' instructions on prayer seem so simple: Ask and you will receive. Praise God. Pray for daily needs. Pray for others. Pray for forgiveness and the strength to forgive. Ask for the strength to stay out of trouble. Give any glory that is yours on earth to God, who is the true recipient of praise and glory.

Think about your attitude towards prayer. Consider Jesus' instructions for prayer and how they can help you move deeper in your prayer life. Examine your prayer life in the remaining silence. Renew your commitment to talking with God regularly. Repeat the phrase "Lord, teach me to pray" until you feel a sense of re-connection with God.

Prayer: "Father, hallowed be thy name. Thy kingdom come. Give us each day our daily bread. And forgive us our sins, as we forgive everyone who is indebted to us. And lead us not into temptation. Draw us to a deeper relationship with you through prayer. Teach us to pray. Amen."

Closing Songs

"In God Alone" (Mon âme se repose), No. 5
"Jesus, Remember Me," No. 7

Loaves and Fishes

Opening Songs

"Sing Praises" (Laudate omnes gentes), No. 13
"Bless the Lord," No. 1
"Lord Jesus Christ" (Jésus le Christ), No. 9

Scripture Reading   Matthew 14:15-16

"As evening approached, the disciples came to him and said, 'This is a remote place, and it's already getting late. Send the crowds away, so they can go to the villages and buy themselves some food.' Jesus replied, 'They do not need to go away. You give them something to eat.'" (NIV)

Something to Think About in the Silence

This miracle is much more than a story about the way Jesus can make big things happen from small means. If you read the story closely, you'll see that it's also a story about the way in which Jesus uses individuals to bless the masses. The disciples didn't know what to do, but Jesus told them to solve the problem of having no food for the large crowd. They basically said to Jesus, "Do something!" But Jesus replied, "You do something!" Jesus told them to gather what they could. Then he blessed it, and there was enough food.

Have you ever been in a situation when you didn't think you had enough, but when you offered what you had to God, it became more than enough? When has God made more out of your little?

Notice how Jesus tells the disciples to do something themselves instead of him just immediately saving the day. Jesus empowers them to go and find what they can and bring it to him. Think about that for a minute. A problem arises, and the disciples demand that Jesus do something, especially since they are accustomed to his performing miracles at will. But this time Jesus doesn't immediately solve the problem. He tells the *disciples* to do something—in other words, he tells them to participate in his miraculous work. The disciples become part of this miracle by gathering what they can.

Can you imagine Jesus inviting you to become part of his work in the world? Plenty of hungry crowds exist today in every country. What can you gather and offer to God that could become a gift to a community in need?

Besides being a story of Jesus' miraculous power, this Scripture passage is a message of empowerment and urgency to minister to others. We can enter the story by asking God to bless our efforts as we work to feed the hungry, clothe the naked, heal the sick, visit prisoners—as we participate in the work of the Kingdom. When Jesus says to you, "Do something," what is he asking you to do?

Prayer: "Jesus, your work is miraculous. Help us to enter your story by gathering and offering our efforts to your glory. Empower us to be a part of your kingdom work in this world. Show us where we can help and give us the courage to do so. Let us be part of your story. Amen."

Closing Songs

"Stay With Us" (Bleib mit deiner Gnade), No. 14
"Our Darkness" (La ténèbre), No. 12
"Let Your Servant Now Go in Peace" (Nunc Dimittis), No. 8

10 Mutual Love

Opening Songs

"Stay With Us" (Bleib mit deiner Gnade), No. 14
"Come and Fill" (Confitemini Domino), No. 3
"Jesus, Remember Me," No. 7

Scripture Reading   Hebrews 13:1-3; 5-8

"Let mutual love continue. Do not neglect to show hospitality to strangers, for by doing that some have entertained angels without knowing it. Remember those who are in prison, as though you were in prison with them; those who are being tortured, as though you yourselves were being tortured. . . . Keep your lives free from the love of money, and be content with what you have; for he has said, 'I will never leave you or forsake you.' So we can say with confidence, 'The Lord is my helper; I will not be afraid. What can anyone do to me?' Remember your leaders, those who spoke the word of God to you; consider the outcome of their way of life, and imitate their faith. Jesus Christ is the same yesterday and today and forever."

Something to Think About in the Silence

Mutual love is also referred to as brotherly love (or sisterly love). This passage tells us not to forget to love. It seems odd that we could forget to love others, but think about the feeling of being satisfied with what you have. Sometimes we can become too content with our lives and forget about those who are in desperate need—both physical and spiritual.

Can you think of a time when you became so absorbed in what you had that you forgot about others in need? It can happen to even the most committed Christians.

Read this passage again and pay close attention to the instructions: Love one another. Be kind to strangers. Remember the imprisoned. Don't love your money too much. Remember those who taught you the Christian faith and model them.

The Letter to the Hebrews was written to a group of people who were being persecuted for believing in Jesus Christ. They knew what it meant to suffer and be imprisoned for their beliefs. The author encouraged them to stay strong and love one another.

What does your community of faith look like? Do you love one another with mutual love? Do you suffer together when one among you is hurting? Do you show kindness to strangers and newcomers to your group? Do you show appreciation for and trust in your leaders? Do you live in the knowledge that God will never abandon you?

Read the passage again. Meditate on the mutual love in your group. Spend the remaining time praying in silence for those in your faith community.

Prayer: "O God, who will never leave or forsake us, hear our prayer. Forgive us for neglecting to show love to all of your children. Give us pure hearts to trust and follow you. Let us say with confidence that you are our God; we will not be afraid. Amen."

Closing Songs

"O Lord, Hear My Prayer," No. 11
"Lord Jesus Christ" (Jésus le Christ), No. 9

11 Breakfast With Jesus

Opening Songs

"Stay With Us" (Bleib mit deiner Gnade), No. 14
"In God Alone" (Mon âme se repose), No. 5
"By Night" (De noche iremos), No. 2

Scripture Reading   John 21:3-7, 9-12a

"Simon Peter said to them, 'I am going fishing.' They said to him, 'We will go with you.' They went out and got into the boat, but that night they caught nothing. Just after daybreak, Jesus stood on the beach; but the disciples did not know that it was Jesus. Jesus said to them, 'Children, you have no fish, have you?' They answered him, 'No.' He said to them, 'Cast the net to the right side of the boat, and you will find some.' So they cast it, and now they were not able to haul it in because there were so many fish. That disciple whom Jesus loved said to Peter, 'It is the Lord!' . . . When they had gone ashore, they saw a charcoal fire there, with fish on it, and bread. Jesus said to them, 'Bring some of the fish you have just caught.' So Simon Peter went aboard and hauled the net ashore, full of large fish, a hundred fifty-three of them; and though there were so many, the net was not torn. Jesus said to them, 'Come and have breakfast.'"

Something to Think About in the Silence

Poor Peter. He's been through a terrible time. His leader was arrested, tried, tortured, crucified, and, dare he believe it, resurrected! It's just too much to take in, so he's going fishing! Fishing is what he used to do before his life and his hopes got turned upside down. But on this night, even fishing was frustrating. There was nothing in the nets. And who was that wise guy on the shore telling them how to fish, anyway? But OK, humor him, go ahead and throw the nets on the other side.

Can you identify with Peter? Have you ever experienced such feelings?

Whoa! What's this? It's crazy—just like everything else in his life! No, it's the Lord, turning things around again! How can this be?

Peter and the disciples went from the despair of loss to the joy of abundance! Their nets were so filled they could easily have broken, but they held all that Christ had given. In the midst of the craziness, Jesus was there filling their nets, filling their hungers, filling their lives!

But first they had to cast their nets to the other side.

In the midst of your crazy life, are you trusting Jesus?

What would you talk to Jesus about over breakfast?

Prayer: "Jesus, come and fill our hearts. We hunger for the bread of life that you offer. Help us to see you, trust you, and receive all that you offer. Amen."

Closing Songs

"Come and Fill" (Confitemini Domino), No. 3
"Our Darkness"(La ténèbre), No. 12
"In the Lord," No. 6

12 Holy Fire

Opening Songs

"Sing Praises" (Laudate omnes gentes), No. 13
"Our Darkness" (La ténèbre), No. 12
"Wait for the Lord," No. 15

Scripture Reading   Acts 2:1-4, 42-45

"When the day of Pentecost came, they were all together in one place. Suddenly a sound like the blowing of a violent wind came from heaven and filled the whole house where they were sitting. They saw what seemed to be tongues of fire that separated and came to rest on each of them. All of them were filled with the Holy Spirit and began to speak in other tongues as the Spirit enabled them. . . . They devoted themselves to the apostles' teaching and to the fellowship, to the breaking of bread and to prayer. Everyone was filled with awe, and many wonders and miraculous signs were done by the apostles. All the believers were together and had everything in common. Selling their possessions and goods, they gave to anyone as he had need." (NIV)

Something to Think About in the Silence

Read the Scripture passage again slowly. What images come to your mind? It reads like a scene from a movie: violent winds, flames that separated and fell on those gathered, the Holy Spirit filling the people, the sound of people talking in different languages at the same time. What a powerful description of what it means to have the Holy Spirit come upon you.

On that day, the Christian church began. In the remaining verses of chapter 2, Peter preaches, people believe, repent, and get baptized, and so become the church. Note the recap of the practices of the early church: "They devoted themselves to the apostles' teaching and to the fellowship, to the breaking of bread and to prayer . . . the believers had everything in common . . . and gave to everyone in need." These early believers were so overcome by the invitation to become the church that they put everything in a big common pot to make sure that everyone's needs were met. They "devoted" themselves to being the church.

What is your level of love for Christ's church? Are you *devoted*? Do you begrudgingly attend and participate in the church's ministries? Do you give what you have for the sake of meeting everyone's needs?

Imagine what it would be like for the Holy Spirit to come today in the same way the Spirit came upon the early church in the Acts of the Apostles. What would your church look like if each member were so filled with the Holy Spirit that he or she became "devoted" to teaching, study, service, evangelism, and helping those in need?

In the remaining silence, meditate on these questions. Pray that the Holy Spirit would consume you with a holy fire, a passion, to be the church in the world. Renew your commitment to the work of the church.

Prayer: "Holy Spirit, come to us. Consume us with your holy fire. You desire for us to become unified as the church for the sake of healing a hurting world. Fill us with a passion for bringing your kingdom on earth. Amen."

Closing Songs

"Come and Fill" (Confitemini Domino), No. 3
"In the Lord" (El Senyor), No. 6
"Let Your Servant Now Go in Peace" (Nunc Dimittis), No. 8

13 Sing Out My Soul

Opening Songs

"Glory to God" (Gloria), No. 4
"Wait for the Lord," No. 15
"Lord Jesus Christ" (Jésus le Christ), No. 9

Scripture Reading   Luke 1:35-38, 46-49

"The angel answered, 'The Holy Spirit will come upon you, and the power of the Most High will overshadow you. So the holy one to be born will be called the Son of God. Even Elizabeth your relative is going to have a child in her old age, and she who was said to be barren is in her sixth month. For nothing is impossible with God.' 'I am the Lord's servant,' Mary answered. 'May it be to me as you have said.' Then the angel left her. . . . And Mary said: 'My soul glorifies the Lord and my spirit rejoices in God my Savior, for he has been mindful of the humble state of his servant. From now on all generations will call me blessed, for the Mighty One has done great things for me—holy is his name.'" (NIV)

Something to Think About in the Silence

"For nothing is impossible with God." Do you believe that statement? The Christmas story certainly works to prove that God is capable of doing what seems impossible to us. First Elizabeth, in her old age, becomes pregnant with John. Then Mary, an unwed virgin, becomes pregnant with the Savior of the world. Nothing is impossible for God!

Surely Mary wondered why God chose her, especially since she appeared to be such an ordinary young woman. Even as she wrestled with the "why" of being chosen to carry the Messiah, she humbly obeyed and said, "May it be to me as you have said." Some translations say, "Let it be to me according to your word." She basically said, "I don't understand why, but I will obey."

Has God ever called you to do something you didn't understand? How did you respond? Take a minute to reflect on the picture of Mary below. Put yourself in her place. She is young. She is an ordinary teenager in her time. God worked a miracle through her.

When God calls you, will your response be humble obedience like Mary's? Look at her and think about what it must have been like for her and how you can imitate her obedience.

Prayer: "God, for whom nothing is impossible, work miracles through us. Help us to offer ourselves to you in humble obedience. Thank you for the example of Mary, for showing us that you use even ordinary people like us to do big things. Use us Lord. Amen."

Closing Song

"Glory to God" (Gloria), No. 4

Illumination

Opening Songs

"Our Darkness" (La ténèbre), No. 12
"Nothing Can Trouble" (Nada te turbe), No. 10
"O Lord, Hear My Prayer," No. 11

Scripture Reading   1 John 1:5-7, 9-11

"This is the message we have heard from him and proclaim to you, that God is light and in him there is no darkness at all. If we say that we have fellowship with him while we are walking in darkness, we lie and do not do what is true; but if we walk in the light as he himself is in the light, we have fellowship with one another, and the blood of Jesus his Son cleanses us from all sin. . . . If we confess our sins, he who is faithful and just will forgive us our sins and cleanse us from all unrighteousness. If we say that we have not sinned, we make him a liar, and his word is not in us."

Something to Think About in the Silence

Have you ever felt like you were full of darkness? Maybe you have felt like there was darkness all around you, and you didn't know how to get out of it. This Scripture passage can help us focus on what it truly means to have the light of Christ live inside us.

Light and darkness cannot exist at the same time and in the same place. Light exposes what is in the darkness, and darkness is overcome by light. So how can the light of God shine through us into the world? How does God's light remove all of the darkness within us? This passage teaches us that hate cannot exist in the heart at the same time as God's light.

Sometimes we allow our doubts and our darkness to have more hold on our lives than God's light. Think about the ways in which your darkness can speak louder to your life than God's light.

Look around you at the illuminated candles. Reflect on the shadows around the room. How might God's light shine so brightly in your life as to cast a reflection of God's face in the world—a reflection of God?

What do you think of when you read about having "fellowship" with God? I think of fellowship as "hanging out." When we get together for church functions, they usually are called fellowship, but they really mean just eating and being together. So when you think of not having fellowship with God, it means to not be with God, to be separated.

Living in God's light means hanging out with God all the time. It means that God shares in every aspect of our lives—good, bad, triumph, failure, joy, and sorrow. Can you imagine riding the roller coaster of life without God? That would mean letting doubts and darkness speak louder to you than the loving voice of God.

How will you walk in the light? in fellowship with God? while loving others? How will others see the light of Christ in your life?

Prayer: "God of light and all that is bright, help us not to let our doubts and darkness speak to us. When they do, please shine ever brighter into our lives so that we are not overcome. Help us to walk in truth and light. Help us to live in your light and to love others, because your love is the brightest light of all. Shine, Jesus, shine. Amen."

Closing Song

"Lord Jesus Christ" (Jésus le Christ), No. 9

Streams in the Desert

Opening Songs

"Wait for the Lord," No. 15
"Nothing Can Trouble" (Nada te turbe), No. 10
"By Night" (De noche iremos), No. 2

Scripture Reading   Isaiah 41:17-20

"When the poor and needy seek water, and there is none, and their tongue is parched with thirst, I the LORD will answer them, I the God of Israel will not forsake them. I will open rivers on the bare heights, and fountains in the midst of the valleys; I will make the wilderness a pool of water, and the dry land springs of water. I will put in the wilderness the cedar, the acacia, the myrtle, and the olive; I will set in the desert the cypress, the plane and the pine together, so that all may see and know, all may consider and understand, that the hand of the LORD has done this, the Holy One of Israel has created it."

Something to Think About in the Silence

Have you ever felt poor? poor in spirit? poor in material things? poor in relationships? poor in looks or intelligence? The promise of this Scripture is that no matter the source of our poverty, God will provide; and when our lives feel dry and deserted, God promises to bring life abundant.

Imagine living in the place described in this Scripture passage. Visualize desert, dry lands, along with complete and utter thirst. What do you see? What does it feel like? What do you say to God in this place?

Now imagine seeing a stream in the desert . . . trees growing before you . . . life springing up all around you. What is the source of this new life? What does the air smell like as you breathe? What is it like to behold?

As you reflect on the Scripture passage, think about the dry lands in your life. Examine your soul and pray for the rain of God.

Let your heart hear God say to you: "I am your God. I bring water to quench your thirst. I bring life in all abundance to you. Tell everyone that I am the One who brings life."

When you feel poor in any area of your life, call on the One who brings new life to desolation. And when the streams of God flow through your deserts, let your life say to the world that the Holy One of Israel is the Lord.

Prayer: "Holy One of Israel, bring life to our barren lands. Spring forth waters to quench the dryness of our souls. Use us to tell the world that you alone are God. Amen."

Closing Songs

"Our Darkness" (La ténèbre), No. 12
"Bless the Lord," No. 1
"O Lord, Hear My Prayer," No. 11

16 Beatitudes

Opening Songs

"Glory to God" (Gloria), No. 4
"Sing Praises" (Laudate omnes gentes), No. 13
"Wait for the Lord," No. 15

Scripture Reading   Matthew 5:3-11

"Blessed are the poor in spirit, for theirs is the kingdom of heaven. Blessed are those who mourn, for they will be comforted. Blessed are the meek, for they will inherit the earth. Blessed are those who hunger and thirst for righteousness, for they will be filled. Blessed are the merciful, for they will be shown mercy. Blessed are the pure in heart, for they will see God. Blessed are the peacemakers, for they will be called sons of God. Blessed are those who are persecuted because of righteousness, for theirs is the kingdom of heaven." (NIV)

Something to Think About in the Silence

Often times the kingdom of God is referred to as an "upside-down" kingdom. Think about it: In this world we assume that blessing is equal to wealth, that being the first and getting ahead means success, that everyone is for him or herself. But listen to the words of Jesus: Blessed are the poor. . . the meek . . . the pure in heart. His message is the opposite of the messages we hear in today's world.

Imagine a world where the poor are considered blessed? What would that look like?

What would it mean for the meek to inherit the earth?

What if those who hunger and thirst for righteousness were blessed instead of persecuted?

Imagine that the peacemakers of the world were seen as sons and daughters of God. What kind of impact would they have on the world?

Read the Scripture passage again slowly. What is God saying to you through these promises?

Are you poor in spirit? mourning? meek? seeking righteousness? merciful? pure in heart? a peacemaker? persecuted for righteousness' sake?

Put your name in each phrase. For instance, "Blessed is Jenny when she is poor in spirit, for hers is the kingdom of heaven." Experience the assurance that in God's kingdom the last are first and that God's rewards are great in heaven.

Prayer: "God of blessings, turn our lives upside down. When we get caught up in what the world says about who we are, remind us that we are yours alone. When this world clouds our understanding of your goodness, point us to your truth. Bless us, O Lord. Amen."

Closing Songs

"Jesus, Remember Me," No. 7
"Let Your Servant Now Go in Peace" (Nunc Dimittis), No. 8

17 The Greatest Story Ever Told

Opening Songs

"Glory to God" (Gloria), No. 4
"Wait for the Lord," No. 15
"O Lord, Hear My Prayer," No. 11

Scripture Reading   Matthew 1:18-23

"Now the birth of Jesus the Messiah took place in this way. When his mother Mary had been engaged to Joseph, but before they lived together, she was found to be with child from the Holy Spirit. Her husband Joseph, being a righteous man and unwilling to expose her to public disgrace, planned to dismiss her quietly. But just when he had resolved to do this, an angel of the Lord appeared to him in a dream and said, 'Joseph, son of David, do not be afraid to take Mary as your wife, for the child conceived in her is from the Holy Spirit. She will bear a son, and you are to name him Jesus, for he will save his people from their sins.' All this took place to fulfill what had been spoken by the Lord through the prophet: 'Look, the virgin shall conceive and bear a son, and they shall name him Emmanuel,' which means, 'God is with us.'"

Something to Think About in the Silence

What an amazing story! In a dream, Joseph is told that his fiancé is pregnant with the Son of God. Not only that, but the Son of God is coming to save the world from sin. A lot of focus in this story is on the fact that Joseph had to deal with Mary's pregnancy, but imagine what he must have thought about the news that God was coming to earth.

God was coming to earth in the form of a human being to walk with us, feel our pains and struggles, and experience our daily lives. God was coming to forgive our sins and create a way back to God where there had been separation. God was coming to be "with us." That's the amazing part of the story. Sure, it is significant that God chose an ordinary young woman who was a virgin. Yes, it must have been a complete act of faith for Joseph to go along with it and not leave her. Of course, the trek to Bethlehem was long and hard for Mary. And yes, Christ was born in a lowly barn. All of these aspects are important, but they are actually supporting themes in the overall divine drama.

The greatest part of the story is the fact that God chose to come in the first place. How God came is really secondary. The fact that God came is why we are saved today. God came and we can know a peace beyond understanding. God came and we are forgiven. God came and the oppressed and impoverished have a Savior and Advocate. God came—and we will live forevermore.

Think about your favorite part of the Christmas story. Is it the angels? the wise men? the shepherds? the journey to Bethlehem?

Now reflect on God's choosing to come at all—coming to make a way for a restored relationship. What is the significance of the story for you? How will you respond to the greatest story ever told?

Prayer: "God who came to earth, come to us again and again through your Holy Spirit. Be with us even now. Write us into your holy story and help us to live empowered by the truth of our forgiveness and eternal life. Thank you for coming to our world. Welcome, Lord Jesus Christ. Amen."

Closing Songs

"Jesus, Remember Me," No. 7

18 Prophetic Voices

Opening Songs

"Come and Fill" (Confitemini Domino), No. 3
"O Lord, Hear My Prayer," No. 11
"Wait for the Lord," No. 15

Scripture Reading   Jeremiah 1:4-9

"Now the word of the Lord came to me saying, 'Before I formed you in the womb I knew you, and before you were born I consecrated you; I appointed you a prophet to the nations.' Then I said, 'Ah, Lord God! Truly I do not know how to speak, for I am only a boy.' But the Lord said to me, 'Do not say, "I am only a boy"; for you shall go to all to whom I send you, and you shall speak whatever I command you. Do not be afraid of them, for I am with you to deliver you, says the Lord.' Then the Lord put out his hand and touched my mouth; and the Lord said to me, 'Now I have put my words in your mouth.'"

Something to Think About in the Silence

The call of Jeremiah is such a powerful image for those of us who feel like we can't speak or feel we don't have a voice in the world. God assures Jeremiah that God will speak through him. He doesn't have to think of what to say; God will use him to pronounce God's Word to the people.

Jeremiah worries about this calling because he is young. You can imagine that he must think that no one would listen to him. Why would the people believe that he was speaking the word of the Lord when he is just a boy?

Have you noticed that throughout Scripture God chooses unlikely men and women to declare God's messages: the old and young, the healthy and those with disabilities, both men and women. God has work to do through each of us.

Do you believe you have something to say to the world? your community? your friends? your family? Have you found your prophetic voice?

We all may not be called to serve as prophets, but we all have a prophetic voice deep in our hearts. Read the passage again. Imagine God putting a hand on your mouth and giving you words to say.

To whom are you called to speak?

What is God calling you to say?

Surrender today the fears of being too young or timid to speak for the Lord. Take this moment to offer your voice to God as one willing to bring God's Word to the world today as Jeremiah did in his day.

Prayer: "God, give us words to say. Put your hand on our lips and fill our mouths with your words. Where there is injustice, call us to speak. Where there is oppression, let your message flow from our mouths. Where there is hopelessness, fill our speech with words of hope and truth and goodness. We offer ourselves to you. Call out our prophetic voices that we might speak your words with confidence. Amen."

Closing Songs

"In the Lord" (El Senyor), No. 6
"Let Your Servant Now Go in Peace" (Nunc Dimittis), No. 8

19 A Great Help

Opening Songs

"Come and Fill" (Confitemini Domino), No. 3
"Our Darkness" (La ténèbre), No. 12
"Nothing Can Trouble" (Nada te turbe), No. 10

Scripture Reading   Psalm 121

"I lift up my eyes to the hills—from where will my help come? My help comes from the LORD, who made heaven and earth. He will not let your foot be moved; he who keeps you will not slumber. He who keeps Israel will neither slumber nor sleep. The LORD is your keeper; the LORD is your shade at your right hand. The sun shall not strike you by day, nor the moon by night. The LORD will keep you from all evil; he will keep your life. The LORD will keep your going out and your coming in from this time on and forevermore."

Something to Think About in the Silence

While you observe the silence, imagine yourself standing on top of the highest mountain looking up to the heavens. What has brought you to this mountain? For what do you need help from the Lord?

Read the passage slowly and then look at the picture. Call to the Lord and listen for the assurance and peace that God will preserve your going out and your coming in from this time forth and forevermore.

Prayer

One: Hear our prayer, O Lord.

All: We lift our eyes to you, O Lord, maker of heaven and earth.

One: When we can do nothing else but look up,

All: We lift our eyes to you, O Lord, maker of heaven and earth.

One: When we fear that evil is closing in around us,

All: We lift our eyes to you, O Lord, maker of heaven and earth.

One: When we feel lost and alone in this world,

All: We lift our eyes to you, O Lord, maker of heaven and earth. Amen.

Closing Songs

"In God Alone" (Mon âme se repose), No. 5
"Sing Praises" (Laudate omnes gentes), No. 13

A Great Help

20 With Us Always

Opening Songs

"In God Alone" (Mon âme se repose), No. 5
"Stay With Us" (Bleib mit deiner Gnade), No. 14
"Come and Fill" (Confitemini Domino), No. 3

Scripture Reading   John 14:15-18; 25-27

"If you love me, you will obey what I command. And I will ask the Father, and he will give you another Counselor to be with you forever—the Spirit of truth. The world cannot accept him, because it neither sees him nor knows him. But you know him, for he lives with you and will be in you. I will not leave you as orphans; I will come to you . . . . All this I have spoken while still with you. But the Counselor, the Holy Spirit, whom the Father will send in my name, will teach you all things and will remind you of everything I have said to you. Peace I leave with you; my peace
I give you. I do not give to you as the world gives. Do not let your hearts be troubled and do not be afraid." (NIV)

Something to Think About in the Silence

Jesus knows firsthand that humans are capable of hearing his teachings, accepting them, and walking away only to forget them. John 14 and the surrounding chapters are filled with Jesus' words, reminding his believers of what he has taught them, reminding them to remember the lessons, the healings, and the miracles. Because Jesus knows humans are prone to forgetting, he vows to send a Counselor to continually remind us of Jesus' story.

The disciples do not understand what Jesus is talking about. The fellowship, the teachings, the conversations, the miracles, the healings, the friendship—all of that is about to change. The disciples would not know Jesus in the same way they had known him for so long. Before Jesus is crucified and resurrected, he wants to be sure that the disciples are well taken care of and that they will continue the ministries he has begun.

Jesus had a plan to comfort and even nurture the community of believers in his absence. He would send the Holy Spirit to remind them of the truth and to comfort them on their journey after he was gone. Even today, we experience the Holy Spirit reminding us of Jesus' teaching, comforting us, and walking with us.

As is customary with Jesus' teachings, love is equal to obedience. If we love Jesus today, we will demonstrate it by loving God and others, by loving our neighbors as ourselves, by healing the sick, and by caring for the sick, lonely, and oppressed.

Think about this statement: If you love me, you will obey what I command.

Do you love Jesus and thus obey his commands?

How will you love and obey him more?

Prayer: "Lord Jesus Christ, you never leave us. Stay close to us and teach us your ways again and again. Write your commandments on our hearts so that we may fully live them out. Send your Counselor to teach us and remind us of your truth. Give us peace to overcome our troubles and fears. Amen."

Closing Songs

"Stay With Us" (Bleib mit deiner Gnade), No. 14
"Jesus, Remember Me," No. 7
"Lord Jesus Christ" (Jésus le Christ), No. 9
"In the Lord" (El Senyor), No. 6

More Worship Feast Resources

🌸 *Worship Feast: 50 Complete Multi-Sensory Services for Youth.* This comprehensive resource includes services for the various seasons, prayer and healing, discovering your spiritual type, graduates, and many more.
ISBN: 0687063671.

🌸 *Worship Feast: 100 Awesome Ideas for Postmodern Youth.* This resource includes ideas for creating your own services or incorporating multisensory worship elements into your existing services.
ISBN: 0687063574.

🌸 *Worship Feast Dramas: 15 Sketches for Youth Groups, Worship, & More* by Beth Miller. This resource provides a variety of long and short skits that ask serious questions about maintaining a life of faith in a not-so-faith-friendly world.
ISBN: 0687044596.

🌸 *Worship Feast Taizé Songbook.* A companion piece for *Worship Feast: 20 Complete Services,* this resource includes fifteen popular and easy-to-sing Taizé songs that will lead youth and youth workers to a deeper prayer experience.
ISBN: 0687739322.

Visit www.Taizé.fr for additional information.

Meet the Writer

Jenny Youngman has worked with youth for ten years. She is editor of the ABINGDON PRESS WORSHIP FEAST resource line. Jenny recently visited Taizé, France, to deepen her walk with God and learn about the community's meaningful style of prayer and worship. She lives outside of Nashville with her husband Mark and daughter Gracie.